THEMATIC UNIT
Creepy Crawlies

Written by Mary Ellen Sterling

Illustrated by Paula Spence

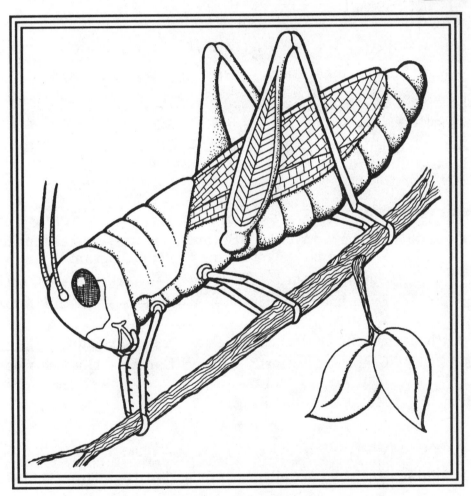

Teacher Created Materials, Inc.
P. O. Box 1214
Huntington Beach, CA 92647
© 1990 Teacher Created Materials, Inc.
Made in U. S. A.

1-55734-268-7

Table Of Contents

Introduction **3**

The Very Hungry Caterpillar by Eric Carle (Putnam, 1969) **5**

Summary —Sample Plan — Overview of Activities — Art Projects — Fruit Graph — Sense Matrix — Story Time Props — Sequence Worksheet — Making a Big Book — See-Through Murals — Butterfly Body Parts — Butterfly Pattern

Over the Steamy Swamp by Paul Geraghty (Harcourt, 1988) **19**

Summary — Sample Plan — Overview of Activities — A Learning Center — Thought Web — Insect Chart — Alike and Opposite — Accordion Book — Life Cycle of a Mosquito

Poetry . . . . **.29**

Chants — Word Bank — Innovations — Cooking — Bug Glasses

Daily Writing Activities . . . . **.35**

Living Charts — Graphing — Graph Books — Sharing Session — Creative Writing Ideas — Bar Graph

Across the Curriculum . . . . **.38**

Language Arts:	Compound Words — Butterfly Treats — Insect Alphabet — Wordsearch — Word Bank — Venn Diagram
Math:	Ant Gameboard — Task Cards — Worksheets — Pencil Poke
Science:	Experiment and Graph — Worksheets — Moth Life Cycle Viewer
Social Studies:	Helpful or Harmful Insects — Insect Friends
Art/Music:	Graph Art Butterfly — Insect Dances — Obstacle Course — Sounds — Shoo, Fly
Life Skills:	Masks — Edible Insects

Culminating Activity . . . . **.66**

Very Important Insect Books — Collage — Honey Treats — Three-D Models

Unit Management . . . . **.68**

Bulletin Board — Awards — Clip Art — Stationery — Invitation — Record Form

Bibliography . . . . **.79**

Answer Key . . . . **.80**

INTRODUCTION

Creepy Crawlies contains a captivating whole language, thematic unit about insects. Its 80 exciting pages are filled with a wide variety of lesson ideas and reproducible pages designed for use with primary children. At its core are two high-quality children's literature selections, *The Very Hungry Caterpillar* and *Over the Steamy Swamp*. For each of these books activities are included which set the stage for reading, encourage the enjoyment of the book, and extend the concepts gained. In addition, the theme is connected to the curriculum with activities in language arts (including daily writing suggestions), math, science, social studies, art, music, and life skills (cooking, physical education, career awareness, etc.) Many of these activities encourage cooperative learning. Suggestions and patterns for bulletin boards and unit management tools are additional time savers for the busy teacher. Futhermore, directions for student-created Big Books and a culminating activity, which allow students to synthesize their knowledge in order to produce products that can be shared beyond the classroom, highlight this very complete teacher resource.

This thematic unit includes:

- ☐ **literature selections** — summaries of two children's books with related lessons (complete with reproducible pages) that cross the curriculum

- ☐ **poetry** — suggested selections and lessons enabling students to write and publish their own works

- ☐ **planning guides** — suggestions for sequencing lessons each day of the unit

- ☐ **writing ideas** — daily suggestions as well as writing activities across the curriculum, including Big Books

- ☐ **bulletin board ideas** — suggestions and plans for student-created and/or interactive bulletin boards

- ☐ **homework suggestions** — extending the unit to the child's home

- ☐ **curriculum connections** — in language arts, math, science, social studies, art, music, and life skills such as cooking, physical education, and career awareness

- ☐ **group projects** — to foster cooperative learning

- ☐ **a culminating activity** — which requires students to synthesize their learning to produce a product or engage in an activity that can be shared with others

- ☐ **a bibliography** — suggesting additional literature and non-fiction books on the theme

> To keep this valuable resource intact so that it can be used year after year, you may wish to punch holes in the pages and store them in a three-ring binder.

INTRODUCTION *(cont.)*

Why Whole Language?

A whole language approach involves children in using all modes of communication: reading, writing, listening, observing, illustrating, experiencing, and doing. Communication skills are interconnected and integrated into lessons that emphasize the whole of language rather than isolating its parts. The lessons revolve around selected literature. Reading is not taught as a separate subject from writing and spelling, for example. A child reads, writes (spelling appropriately for his/her level), speaks, listens, etc. in response to a literature experience introduced by the teacher. In this way, language skills grow naturally, stimulated by involvement and interest in the topic at hand.

Why Thematic Planning?

One very useful tool for implementing an integrated whole language program is thematic planning. By choosing a theme with correlating literature selections for a unit of study, a teacher can plan activities throughout the day that lead to a cohesive, in-depth study of the topic. Students will be practicing and applying their skills in meaningful contexts. Consequently, they will tend to learn and retain more. Both teachers and students will be freed from a day that is broken into unrelated segments of isolated drill and practice.

Why Cooperative Learning?

Besides academic skills and content, students need to learn social skills. No longer can this area of development be taken for granted. Students must learn to work cooperatively in groups in order to function well in modern society. Group activities should be a regular part of school life and teachers should consciously include social objectives as well as academic objectives in their planning. For example, a group working together to write a report may need to select a leader. The teacher should make clear to the students and monitor the qualities of good leader-follower group interaction just as he/she would state and monitor the academic goals of the project.

Why Big Books?

An excellent cooperative, whole language activity is the production of Big Books. Groups of students, or the whole class, can apply their language skills, content knowledge, and creativity to produce a Big Book that can become a part of the classroom library to be read and reread. These books make excellent culminating projects for sharing beyond the classroom with parents, librarians, other classes, etc. Big Books can be produced in many ways and this thematic unit book includes directions for at least one method you may choose.

The Very Hungry Caterpillar

by Eric Carle

Summary

The **Very Hungry Caterpillar** is the story of a caterpillar's metamorphosis into a butterfly. The journey begins with an egg on a leaf. After some time, a caterpillar hatches from the egg. This is no ordinary caterpillar, however; he's a **very hungry** caterpillar! Each day of the week he eats through more and more food until he gets a stomachache. Finally satisfied, he builds a cocoon around himself and remains there for more than two weeks. Then he nibbles his way out of the cocoon and emerges as a beautiful butterfly.

Originally written in 1969, the illustrations were completely redone for the newest edition. Bright, bold colors and collage technique make this book a visual delight. In addition, this story cleverly instructs children as it guides them through the days of the week, sets of up to ten objects, and the transformation of the caterpillar.

The outline below is a suggested plan for using the various activities that are presented in this unit. You should adapt these ideas to fit your own classroom situation.

Sample Plan

Day I

- Daily Writing Activities: Graphing, graph book, sharing session (page 35)
- Make egg carton caterpillars (page 8)
- Put up Caterpillar's Story bulletin board (pages 68-73)
- Read *The Very Hungry Caterpillar* aloud to class
- Essential Comprehension Activity, #4 (page 7)
- Assign homework: bring samples or pictures of fruit

Day II

- Continue Daily Writing Activities
- Share Homework: Classify; recall activities (page 6)
- Essential Comprehension Activity, #5 (page 7)
- Make fruit kebobs (page 7)

- Record responses on a Sense Matrix (page 10)

Day III

- Continue Daily Writing Activities
- Extend Homework: Make a graph (page 9)
- Complete Worksheet: Butterfly Body Parts (page 17)
- Math: Do You Know These Insects? (page 47)

Day IV

- Continue Daily Writing Activities
- Creative Writing Activities (page 36)
- Math: Lady Bug Pencil Poke (page 48) or Insect Math (page 46)
- Art: Tissue Butterflies (page 8)

Day V (may take more than one day)

- Culminating Activity: Big Book (page 15) and See-Through Murals (page 16)

Overview Of Activities

SETTING THE STAGE

1. Make the Caterpillar's Story bulletin board. Have the children make egg carton caterpillars (see page 8). Attach the caterpillars to the bulletin board.

2. Gather the children together so that they are comfortable and can all see the book. Show the title page of the book. Explain that the story is about how a caterpillar changes.

3. Ask the children to predict what events will happen in the story. Record the predictions on the chalkboard or chart paper. Later, compare the predictions with what actually happened in the book.

4. Read the first three pages of the book and then STOP. Tell the children some foods you would look for if you were hungry. Let a few children volunteer their favorite foods. Then have them turn to their neighbor and exchange favorite food ideas. This allows all children to become actively involved and provides opportunity for oral communication.

ENJOYING THE BOOK

1. As you read the book, STOP after each day and have the children predict the day of the week and what the very hungry caterpillar will eat next.

2. **Homework Activity:** Have each child bring an actual fruit or pictures of fruits. Use the fruit to complete one or more of the following activities:

   Classify the fruits according to shape, size, and color. Extend this project with a follow-up graphing worksheet (see page 9). Pair students to complete the graphs.

   Line up three or four fruits or fruit pictures on the chalkboard tray. Direct the children to close their eyes while you remove one. Have students open their eyes and tell which is missing. Or, while the students have their eyes closed, rearrange the fruit or fruit pictures; let a student put them back in their original order. A third option is to display five or six fruits or pictures of fruit. Take all of them away. Students must list them.

   If actual fruit (fresh, canned, or frozen) is collected, have the children cut the fruit into chunks and then thread an assortment of fruit on wooden skewers. Use all senses to describe the fruits. In small groups, have students record their responses on a Sense Matrix (see page 10).

Overview Of Activities *(cont.)*

3. Put each egg carton caterpillar into a brown paper bag cocoon and "hang" from the tree branches of the bulletin board. (To make bags resemble cocoons, scrunch them up and then unravel them.)

   Leave them for ten to fourteen days; count down on the calendar. In the meantime, make the tissue butterflies (page 8). On the last day of the countdown, remove the bags from the bulletin board and replace with the tissue butterflies. Hang or display some butterflies in other areas of the room.

4. **Essential Comprehension Activity:** Suspend a clothesline across a wall or in a safe place in the classroom. Prepare the story time props from pages 11 to 13. Pass out the props among the students. As you read the story, have the children hang the props on the clothesline. An alternate way to use the props is to attach a craft stick to each one. Give each child a prop. Then have the students arrange themselves in the order in which they appear in the story.

5. **Another Essential Comprehension Activity:** Sequencing events. Allow students to work with a partner to complete the A Very Busy Week For Caterpillar worksheet (page 14). Use the sentence strips to create a Big Book.

EXTENDING THE BOOK

1. Make a Big Book. See pages 15 and 16 for complete directions.

2. See-Through Murals. Use as pages for a Big Book or for illustrating facts about insects. Page 16 gives complete directions for construction of these unusual art projects.

3. Learn about butterflies. (Use Butterfly Body Parts, page 17.)

4. Write and attach butterfly shape stories to bulletin board. Use the pattern on page 18.

Art Projects

Egg Carton Caterpillar

Materials:

- Egg carton cut into sections of three; powdered green tempera paint; paint brushes; gummed paper or marking pen; pipe cleaners; glue; cotton balls.

Directions:

- Paint the egg carton section green.
- After the egg carton has dried, glue a green cotton ball to the top of each section. (Color the cotton balls by shaking them in green powdered tempera paint.)
- Draw eyes or use gummed paper.
- Poke two holes in the caterpillar's head; attach a section of pipe cleaner to each hole.

Tissue Butterflies

Materials:

Wax paper; liquid starch; paintbrushes; colored tissue paper cut in two or three-inch squares (5 or 7.5 cm); butterfly pattern (see page 18); string.

Directions:

- Place a butterfly pattern on a flat surface; cover with a sheet of wax paper.
- Paint the tissue paper squares onto the wax paper with the liquid starch. Follow the outline of the butterfly; fill in completely.
- Make two to three layers of tissue; dry overnight.
- Carefully peel away the wax paper.
- Thread a length of string through the top of the butterfly and hang it from the ceiling. Or, tape the butterflies to a window for a stained glass effect. Or, pin to the Caterpillar's Story bulletin board after the ''cocoons have opened.''

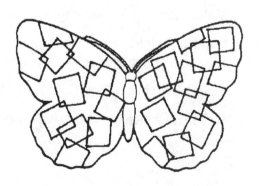

8

Name:	Date:

Fruit Graph

Display the fruits on a table. Draw or write the name of one fruit in each rectangle. Then answer the questions below. *(See page 6 for more directions.)*

number of fruits	Red	Yellow	Blue	Orange	Purple	Green
10						
9						
8						
7						
6						
5						
4						
3						
2						
1						

1. Most of the fruits are which color? _____

2. Which colors have the same number of fruits? _____
_____

3. How many fruits are there altogether? _____

4. Were any colors left out? Which one(s)? _____

5. Name some other fruits that were not brought to class. Tell what colors they are. _____

Name:		Date:			

Sense Matrix

(See page 6 for directions.)

Tastes					
Feels					
Sounds					
Smells					
Looks					
FRUIT					

10

Story Time Props

Color, cut out, and glue to tagboard. Laminate for durability. Staple a craft stick to the bottom of the shape if desired. Patterns can be enlarged with an overhead projector.

Story Time Props *(cont.)*

12

Story Time Props *(cont.)*

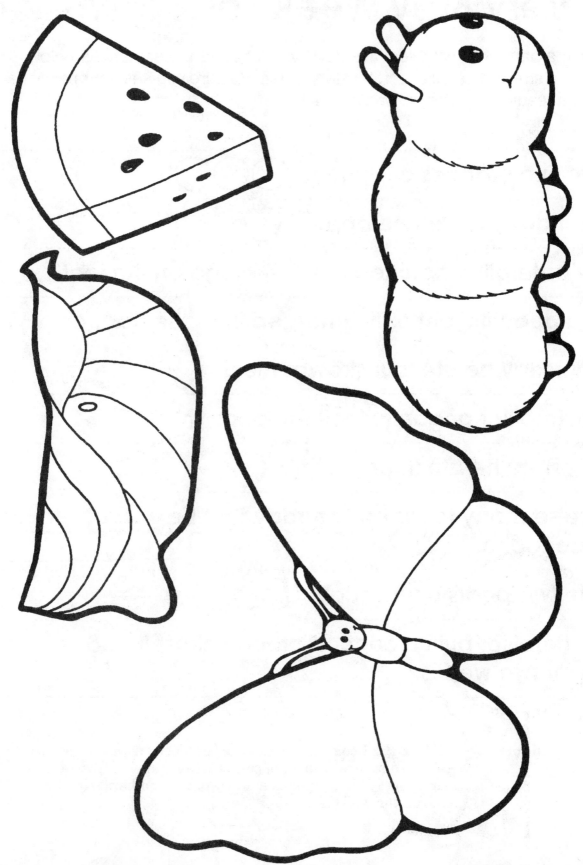

Name:	Date:

A Very Busy Week For Caterpillar

Work with a partner to complete this activity. Cut apart the sentences below. Paste them onto a sheet of paper in correct story order. Be sure you and your partner agree. Take turns reading the story to one another.

Cut on dotted lines.

He ate five oranges on Friday.

On Monday he ate one apple.

A tiny caterpillar hatched out of the egg on the leaf.

Then a beautiful butterfly emerged from the cocoon.

On Thursday he ate four strawberries.

The caterpillar began to look for food.

Wednesday he ate three plums.

He ate so many foods on Saturday that he got a stomachache.

He ate two pears on Tuesday.

The caterpillar built a cocoon around himself and stayed there for two weeks.

Extension: Make a Big Book. Cut apart the sentence strips above. Glue each to a separate sheet of construction paper. Illustrate each page. Put the pages in story order and hang side by side on the walls.

Making A Big Book

This cooperative group project is a culminating activity for the story of the very hungry caterpillar. It combines language, reading, writing and art to provide a variety of methods which will encourage and motivate creative processes.

Once the children are thoroughly familiar with a book, they can create an innovation (a change in the character, setting, or events of a story) by following the steps below. Small groups can work together to rewrite and illustrate their own stories.

- **Rehearse** several possibilities of how the story might be changed. For example, the very hungry caterpillar might become the very hungry ant. The fruits might be changed to sugary foods. Discuss a new twist for the ending—the ant might grow too big to fit into the tunnel to his home.

- **Write** the entire language pattern on an overhead projector or on chart paper. Leave blanks where you want to change words.
  Example: A very hungry _____ began to look for _____.

- **Brainstorm** and make a Word Bank of all the words that could be used in the blank spaces.

- **Direct** students to select words from the Word Bank to use in filling in the blanks.

- **Make** language strips; have the children copy a chunk of text onto each strip.

- **Illustrate** the text by making a see-through mural (see page 16 for complete directions).

- **Hang** the mural pages end-to-end on a clothesline or windows so that students can read both sides of the murals.

See-Through Murals

These art projects can be made any size, but larger ones are more impressive. A variety of materials should be available for the students to choose from.

Materials

Clear self-adhesive paper; construction paper; crayons or markers; scissors; any of the following items: art tissue, fabric scraps, colored acetate, wallpaper samples, printed wrapping paper, aluminum foil, yarn, magazines and newspapers.

Directions

- Write a sentence or two on both sides of a 4 x 8-inch (10 x 20 cm) piece of construction paper.

- Illustrate the text using a variety of mediums. Cut out all shapes and assemble in the design you want.

- Cut two 25 x 8-inch (62.5 x 20 cm) sheets of the self-adhesive paper. Carefully peel the backing from one sheet.

- Lay sticky side up on a flat surface.

- Place the sentence strip at the bottom of the paper.

- Now assemble all the pieces onto the paper.

- When the picture is complete, peel the backing from the other sheet of self-stick paper.

- Two persons should lay the paper sticky side down onto the picture.

- Trim the edges if necessary.

- After all pages are completed hang them end-to-end on the windows or a clothesline for the students to read. Later, they can be joined with rings or yarn to make a Big Book to add to the classroom library.

The very hungry ant began to look for food.

Name:	Date:

Butterfly Body Parts

There are many parts to a butterfly. Trace the words below. Color the picture.

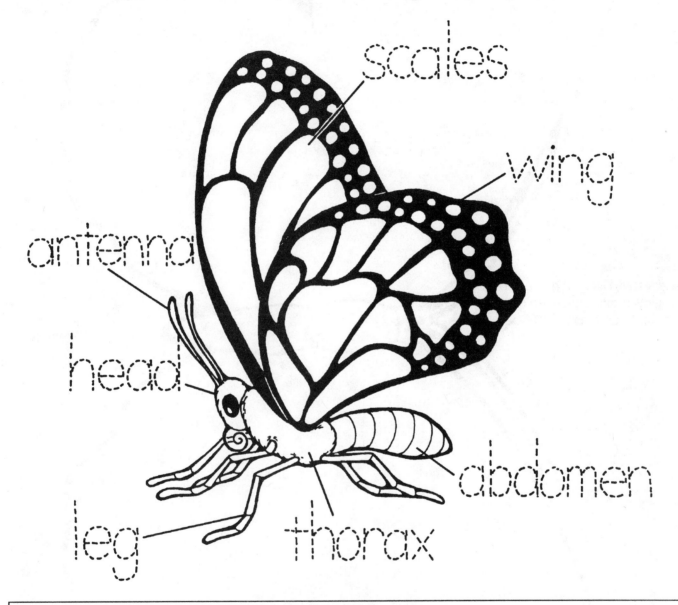

Some Butterfly Facts

Count and write the number.

1.   A butterfly has _____ legs.

2.   A butterfly has _____ body parts — the head, thorax, and abdomen.

3.   A butterfly has _____ wings and _____ antennae.

The Very Hungry Caterpillar

Butterfly Pattern

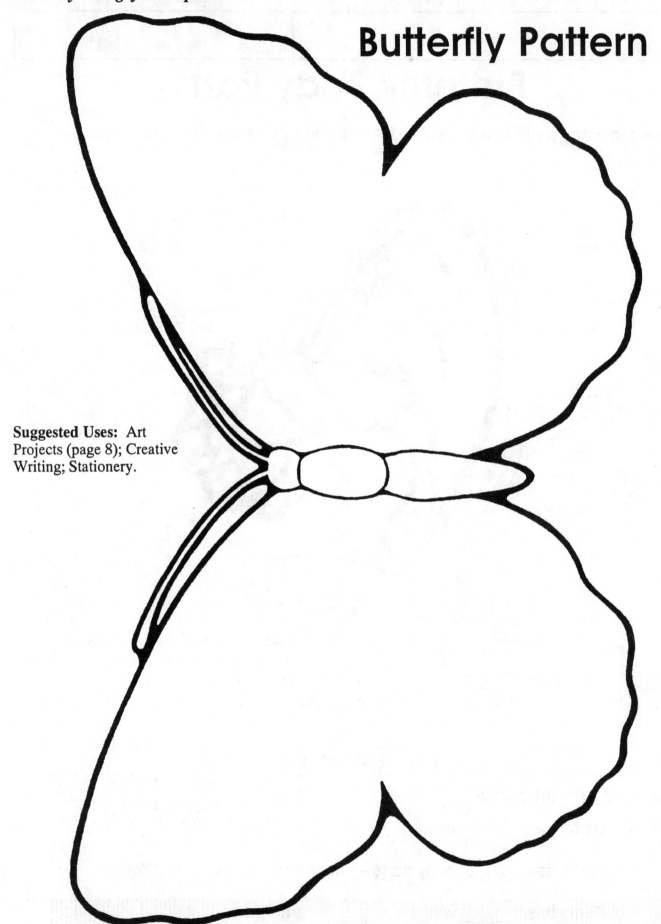

Suggested Uses: Art
Projects (page 8); Creative
Writing; Stationery.

Over the Steamy Swamp

by Paul Geraghty

SUMMARY

One steamy afternoon, a tired and hungry mosquito flies over a quiet swamp. A greedy dragonfly watches as the mosquito goes by. Watching the dragonfly is a famished frog. Watching the frog is a peckish fish. And so the story goes as the mosquito continues on his flight over the silent swamp.

Alliterative descriptions and colorful caricatures make this book particularly eye-appealing. The reader will be delighted with the humorous eye-catching drawings and the text will satisfy the most voracious appetite for words. Told in a cumulative style, this story explores the predator-prey relationship in a most entertaining manner.

The outline below is a suggested plan for using the various activities that are presented in this unit. You should adapt these ideas to fit your own classroom situation.

Sample Plan

DAY I

- Daily Writing Activities: graphing, graph book, sharing session (page 35)
- Brainstorm Swamp: make a thought web (page 23)
- Read *Over the Steamy Swamp* aloud to whole class
- Essential Comprehension Activity, #4 (page 21)
- Complete Worksheet: Insect Parts (page 52)
- Assign Homework: Insect Chart (page 24)

DAY II

- Continue Daily Writing Activities
- Share Homework: Classify insects, make charts (page 20)
- Essential Comprehension Activity, #5 (page 21)
- Vocabulary Worksheet: Alike and Opposite (page 25)
- Art Project: Collage (page 67)

- Swamp Obstacle course (page 62)

DAY III

- Continue Daily Writing Activities
- Extend Homework: Make an Insect/Not Insect Chart (page 20)
- Complete Worksheet: Did You Know...? (page 49)
- Create Own Insects (page 36)
- Make Edible Insects (page 65)

DAY IV

- Continue Daily Writing Activities
- Make an Accordion Book (page 26)
- Science: Life Cycle of a Mosquito (pages 27 and 28)
- Complete Worksheets: Insect Math (page 46)
- Write Insect Chants (page 29)

DAY V

- Culminating Activity: Very Important Insects Book (page 66)

OVERVIEW OF ACTIVITIES

SETTING THE STAGE

1. Set the mood in the room with an appropriate bulletin board, poster display, and/or a Learning Center (see page 22 for how-to's on creating a Learning Center).

2. At the Learning Center stock books — both factual and fiction —about insects; a basket or plastic crate makes an appealing container for the texts. See page 79 for some suggested titles.

3. Create an Insect Viewer. Place an old log or tree limb inside an aquarium. Take the students on a nature walk to collect some insects. Place the bugs inside the aquarium. Cover with clear plastic wrap; poke some air holes in the plastic. Keep a supply of paper, pencils, and various art supplies next to the viewer so that children can record insect activity in both written and art form.

4. Brainstorm with the whole class. Write the word *swamp* on the chalkboard or on chart paper. Make a web of words—animals, sights, and sounds—that might be associated with the swamp (for how-to's on webbing see page 23).

5. Explain that the book you are going to read takes place in a swamp. Direct children to listen carefully as you read the story for any of the words that are on their brainstorming list.

ENJOYING THE BOOK

1. Pause at the end of each page and allow the students to predict an animal the mosquito might not notice next. Also have the students predict what will happen when the mosquito bites the lion. After reading the whole book, compare the illustrations and descriptions of the mosquito on the first and last pages. What changes do you see? Why?

2. **Learn about Insects:** Have students complete the Insect Parts worksheet page 52. As they work in pairs, encourage them to use the insect books from the Learning Center. *Bugs* is an excellent resource for this activity. (See the Bibliography, page 79, for more titles.)

3. **Homework Activity:** Complete an Insect chart (see page 24 for a sample). Activities using the completed charts include classifying the insects according to where they live, what they eat, size, day or night insects, insects that sting or bite, etc. Assign small groups a classification. Have them make a chart of insects in that category. They can draw or cut out pictures from books or magazines to go with their text. (An excellent resource for this activity is *Insects Do the Strangest Things*. See Bibliography page 79.)

   Homework Activity: Make Insect/Not Insect Charts. Have students use animals from *Over the Steamy Swamp* as well as words from the class web.

OVERVIEW OF ACTIVITIES *(cont.)*

4. **Essential Comprehension Activity:** Reread the book, asking children to note the order in which the animals appear. On index cards or rectangular pieces of construction paper write the names of all the characters in the book *Over the Steamy Swamp*. Pass out the cards to various students. Direct them to line themselves in order of their appearance in the first half of the story. In turn let them explain who they are and who comes next. Collect the cards and give them to different students. These students must arrange themselves in order from the middle of the story, where the mosquito bites the lion, to the end. Have them act out their reactions as they go down the line.

5. **Another Essential Comprehension Activity:** With yarn, make a stairway outline with nine steps on each side of a central peak representing the climax or high point of the story. Assign a different character and scene to each child to illustrate. After all the pictures have been drawn, the students are to put their pictures on the steps in story sequence order. Have each child explain what is happening in his picture.

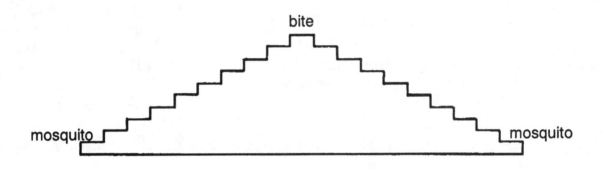

6. **Vocabulary:** *Over the Steamy Swamp* is filled with descriptive phrases and colorful language. One fun activity using this vocabulary can be found on page 25.

EXTENDING THE BOOK

1. Make an Accordion Book (see page 26): First, rehearse ways to change the story. For example, a new setting might be the Festive Forest. Characters could include caterpillars, ants, flies, rabbits, etc. Then students write their own cumulative stories in small groups. Make sure they include at least one insect in their story.

2. **Science - The Life Cycle of a Mosquito:** On pages 27 and 28 students first put the events of the mosquito's life cycle in order. Then they build a viewer so they can focus on one step at a time.

Creating A Learning Center

A Learning Center is a special area set aside in the classroom for the study of a specific topic. Typically, a Learning Center contains a variety of activities and materials that teach, reinforce, and enrich skills and concepts. Because students learn in different ways and at different rates, a Learning Center can be a valuable means of providing for these differences. Activities in a given center should be based on the abilities, needs, and interests of the students in your classroom. Learning Centers are equally appropriate for cooperative group and individual use.

How to Create a Learning Center

- Select a theme or topic in any subject area, e.g. Creepy Crawlies.

- Label the center attractively with a display or poster.

- Determine specific skills or concepts to be taught or reinforced; e.g., the body parts of an insect, identify insects, compare moths and butterflies.

- Develop appropriate learning activities; e.g., life cycle viewer, bug gameboard, science experiments.

- Prepare extended activities for reinforcement or enrichment; e.g., worksheets, art activities (bug glasses, see-through murals, 3-D models), creative writing (chants, poems, insect alphabet).

- Gather all materials needed to complete the projects at this center, e.g. books, art supplies, paper and pencils.

Scheduling Center Time

- Plan a rotating schedule where groups of children are rotated to different activities. For example, one group can be attending a teacher-directed lesson, while the second group completes seat work, and the third group is at the Learning Center.

- Assign individuals or small groups to the center according to diagnosed needs.

- Have a set Center Time each day. Assign a different group each day to work at the center during that time.

Record Keeping

- Use a simple Record Form (see page 78) to record all students names and check off as they complete a particular project.

- Make a monthly calendar for each student; store in a three-ring binder at the center. Record information on the appropriate spaces.

- Keep a file box with students' names listed alphabetically on index cards. Record notes and activities completed on the cards.

22

How To Make A Thought Web

A web can be used to help students organize their thoughts and to determine what they know about a topic. Webbing is a cooperative process for determining all possible directions and activities to explore on a particular topic.

To begin a web, suggest a theme and record it in the center space. Encourage students to brainstorm ideas, questions and related topics. As they do so, record their responses on rays drawn from the central space. Use the same color marking pen or chalk throughout this initial activity. As a follow-up or assessment activity, review this initial web and, with a different color pen or chalk, check off those things covered in your lessons.

Although webs can be created with the whole class, they are also a good activity for small cooperative groups to work on. Display the webs throughout the unit of study. They can be used as Word Banks for creative writing, references for factual information, and as tools for assessment. Webs can be added to at any time and provide a quick visual reference for progress checks.

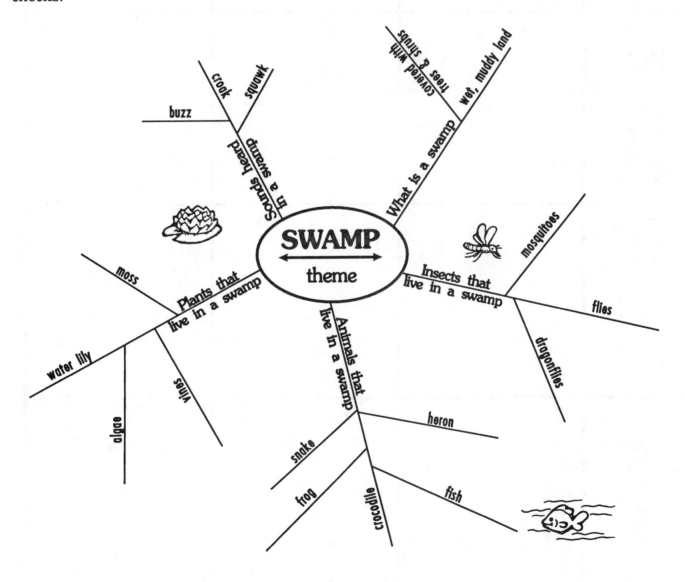

Name:		Date:	

Insect Chart

An Interesting Fact			
Where it Lives			
What it Eats			
Insect Name			

Name: _____   Date: _____

Alike...

Describe each character below with a synonym for the **bold** word. (Synonyms are words that mean the same). Use the **SYNONYM WORD BANK** to help you.

1. **ravenous** lion __ **t** __ __ __ __ __ __ __

2. **cowering** crocodile __ __ __ __ __ **f** __ __

3. **peckish** fish __ __ __ **g** __ __ __

4. **stealthy** snake __ __ __ __ __ __ **y** __

5. **hostile** hunter __ __ **f** __ __ __ __ __ __ __

6. **flabbergasted** frog __ __ __ **r** __ __ __ __ __ __

SYNONYM WORD BANK

fearful
surprised
sneaky
starving
unfriendly
hungry

and Opposite

full
lazy
friendly
generous
alert
tiny

Describe each character below with an antonym for the **bold** word. (Antonyms are words that mean the opposite). Use the **ANTONYM WORD BANK** to help you.

1. **hostile** hunter __ __ **r** __ __ __ __ __ __

2. **greedy** dragonfly __ __ **n** __ __ __ __ __

3. **tired** mosquito __ __ __ __ **r** __

4. **busy** fish __ __ **a** __ __ __

5. **famished** frog __ __ __ **l** __

6. **big** lion __ __ __ **n** __

ANTONYM WORD BANK

How To Make An Accordion Book

Accordion books can be created in small cooperative groups or by individuals. Life cycles, poetry, and step-by-step directions are especially suited for accordion books. Complete directions and materials are listed below. If the book needs to be longer, make another book and attach it with tape to the end of the book.

Materials:

Butcher paper; cardboard or tagboard; writing paper; crayons, marking pens, or any other art supplies needed to make illustrations.

Directions:

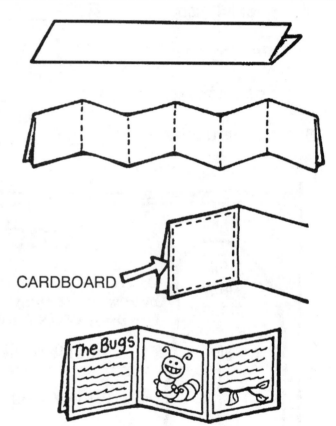

- Fold butcher paper in half lengthwise for strength.

- Divide and fold the paper into an even number of sections.

- Insert a piece of tagboard or cardboard into each end to make the book stand up easily. Tape the ends together.

CARDBOARD

- Put the text and illustrations on separate paper. Glue one page to each section of the accordion book.

- Give the accordion book more character by making a shape cover. If the book is about caterpillars, for example, attach a caterpillar face to the front of the cover and a "tail" to the back cover.

26

Life Cycle Of A Mosquito

In the story *Over the Steamy Swamp* a hungry mosquito hunts for food. Find out more about the mosquito by making this picture frame.

Directions

- Cut out around the bold lines of the pictures and sentence strip on page 28. Glue the pictures in order onto the sentence strip.

- Glue to tagboard or construction paper for more durability, if desired.

- Cut slits on the dashed lines of the frame below.

- Insert Tab B of the picture/sentence strip from behind the frame and through the top slit.

- Then slide Tab B through the bottom slit.

- Pull down on Tab B until the first picture is visible in the frame.

- Pull up on Tab A to move the pictures one frame at a time.

- **Extension:** Have small groups make their own frame and sentence strip to explain the life cycle of another insect.

Cut along the bold lines.

Life Cycle

- -

- -

of a Mosquito

frame for life cycle viewer

Life Cycle Of A Mosquito

(cont.)

In a week, the wriggler changes into a pupa which floats just under the water.

In a few days the pupa's skin splits down the back. A winged adult mosquito comes out.

First, the female mosquito drops her eggs in water.

A wriggler hatches from each egg. It eats tiny animals in the water.

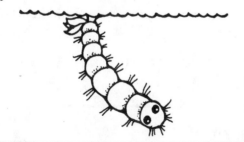

TAB A

SENTENCE STRIP

TAB B

Insect Chants

This mini-unit can be used anytime during the Creepy Crawlies unit. It can easily be adapted to a particular insect that you would like to study. During this unit, students will learn a simple chant, write and illustrate their own chant, and perform their chant for the class.

Writing an Insect Chant

1. Duplicate the Insect Chant or write the chant on the chalkboard or on an overhead projector; have students copy the words.

2. Read the words together. Model the chant for the students. Then have the students chant together. Be sure to place the accent on the **bold faced** words.

Insect Chant
*Insects in the **yard***
*Naming them's not **hard***
*Insects **black**, insects **green**,*
*Insects **nice** and insects **mean**!*

3. Brainstorm with the class. Discuss the different insects they have seen and create a Word Bank on chart paper or the overhead projector.

Insect Word Bank		
Size	**What they do**	**Where they live**
tiny minute small	fly crawl jump bite	near swamps on dogs and cats in gardens in houses

4. Make a chart of the worksheet on page 32 or display on an overhead projector. With the whole group model filling in the blanks by using the Insect Word Bank.

5. Pair students in workable pairs. Have them create their own chants. They may use words from the Insect Word Bank or brainstorm other words.

Insect Chants *(cont.)*

More Poems

1. Read this poem to the whole group:

   "And what's a butterfly? At best,
   He's but a caterpillar, dressed."
   John Gay, 1727

   Have them choose other insect names to use in the poem.

2. Sing or read *"I Know an Old Lady Who Swallowed a Fly."* Brainstorm insect names and actions. Then have students make up their own initial lyric. For example, "I know an old lady who swallowed a bee; it buzzed and buzzed and couldn't get free." Direct the students to write their lyrics on paper strips. One at a time, have the students read their poem and then place it in the Old Lady's mouth to be collected in a shoe box placed behind the cut-out (see page 33).

3. Although the "Eensy Weensy Spider" is not about an insect, insect names could be substituted for "spider" and different action words could be used to replace those in the rhyme. Have students recite their new rhymes.

4. Mother Goose rhymes provide a fun springboard for creating innovations. Here's a Mother Goose rhyme that could easily be innovated:

   ### There Was a Bee
   *There was a **bee***
   *Sat on a **wall***
   *And **"Buzz!"** said he*
   And that was all.

   Replace the underlined words with different insect names, action words, etc. A sample rewrite:

   There was a moth
   Chewed on some cloth
   "Yum!" said the moth,
   "Now I'll have broth."

Insect Chants *(cont.)*

Art Activity

Make Bug Glasses (see page 34 for complete directions). Have the students wear their bug glasses as they present their original Insect Chants to the class.

Class Chant Book

After the students have written and illustrated their chants, make a cover and bind all the pages together. Add it to the classroom library.

Share it with another class.

Cooking Activity

Make edible insects! You will find delicious recipes on page 65.

Insect Riddles

Brainstorm with the class and list the insects on the chalkboard or a chart. Next to each insect, make a list of words that rhyme with that name. Group students and have them write riddles about insects using words from the Word Bank. For example, "What insect made Rick's dog sick? A tick." (More insect riddles can be found in the book **Bugs** by Nancy Winslow Parker and Joan Richards Wright, Mulberry Books, New York, 1987.) Have the students share their riddles with the class.

Poems

Read some poems about insects (***The Random House Book of Poetry for Children*** contains a lively variety of insect poems.) A good example is "Wasps" by Dorothy Aldis. Direct the students to write innovations of the poem. Brainstorm with the whole group and make a Word Bank of other insects that could be used for the title. Then list other foods that could be substituted for the ones in the poem "Wasps."

Name:	Date:

Insect Chant

With a partner write an insect chant together. Draw a picture in the box below.

Written and illustrated by:

_____

_____

Insect Chant

Insects in the yard.

Naming them is not hard.

Insects_____, insects_____,

Insects_____

and insects_____.

I Know An Old Lady

Color, cut and glue to tagboard. Cut out the mouth. Attach to end of a shoe box.

• See page 30 for suggested activities.

Bug Glasses

After the students have written their chants, let them make their own bug glasses to go along with their writing. Then they can wear their bug glasses as they present their chant to the class.

Materials:

Egg carton cups cut in sections of two attached; scissors; pencil; pipe cleaners; aluminum foil, colored markers, tempera paint, self-stick colored dots or stars, stickers, construction paper, etc. for decoration.

Directions:

- Cut out the bottoms of the egg cups to make eye holes.
- Paint the outside of the cups with tempera paint; make any kind of designs and colors as desired. Let dry.
- Or instead of painting the egg cups, cover them completely with aluminum foil. Be sure to remove the foil from the eye holes.
- With a pencil, poke a hole in the outside of each cup — one hole on the left side and one hole on the right side.
- Attach a pipe cleaner to each hole. Bend the pipe cleaners to fit around the ears.
- Decorate the bug glasses with stars, stickers, construction paper, etc.

Suggested Uses:

- Have the students wear their bug glasses as they present their Insect Chants to the class.
- Hold a Best Bug Glasses contest. Students can enter categories such as Silliest, Most Realistic, or Most Decorated. Give awards (see page 74 for a sample one). Another class or teacher can act as judge for this contest.
- Play a "Who Am I?" game. One child is chosen to be an insect (the teacher can assign an insect or the child can choose his own); he wears his bug glasses and sits in front of the group. The rest of the class tries to guess his identity by asking appropriate "yes" or "no" questions. For example, "Are you green?" "Do you make honey?" "Do you live underground?"

34

Daily Writing Activities

Living Charts

To make a "living" wall chart, put strips of masking tape turned over onto itself on the wall or chalkboard. (Double-stick tape may be used instead of masking tape.) Place the strips vertically or horizontally. Or, attach parallel lines of yarn to the wall; keep a supply of clothepins in a basket next to the yarn lines.

Graphing

Before the students arrive each day, write a question and place it above the "living" chart. Students can use self-stick notes for name tags or make their own picture to go up on the chart. Direct the class to form a line and then one person at a time places their name or picture on the chart. As they do so, they can explain their choice.

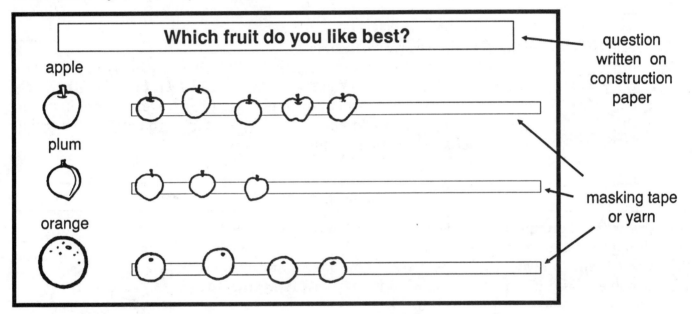

Which fruit do you like best?

apple

plum

orange

question written on construction paper

masking tape or yarn

Graph Book

Fold a large sheet of construction paper in half. Insert copies of the blank bar graph (page 37) into the fold; staple. Have each child make a booklet in this same manner and allow time on the first day to decorate the cover. Every day students are to make bar graphs based on the data gathered during the initial graphing activity. While students are engaged in making their graphs, you can take attendance or collect homework or get lunch counts, etc. Note: You may pre-determine the title of the graph or allow students to create their own.

Sharing Session

Encourage speaking and listening skills by dividing the students into small groups of three to five. Each person takes a turn sharing their graphs with the group. This can be done on a daily or a weekly basis. It is a good confidence builder plus it provides children with a chance to know one another better.

Writing Activities *(cont.)*

An alternative to the graphing and charting ideas on the previous page is to have students write on a different topic every day. You can give students a choice of topics or assign a specific one each day. Or, give students a deadline by which they must complete writings on every subject. They can be done individually or worked on cooperatively in pairs and small groups.

Bug Caricatures

Everyone knows what a rubber band is, yet if we interpret the words literally we can just imagine pieces of rubber playing instruments! Have students draw pictures and write about these insects:

ladybug, firefly, dragonfly, lightning bug, potato bug, etc.

What If...?

Have students write a short story that tells how things may appear from an insect's point of view. (You may want to read **Two Bad Ants** by Chris Van Allsburg to the class.) For example, what if you were an ant carrying a crystal of sugar over a kitchen counter? Or what if you were a flea trying to jump across a puddle in a busy street?

Create an Insect

In pairs or small groups have students think up a new insect name by combining the names of two insects, e.g. butterfly + flea = butterflea. Then tell them to draw a picture of their new insect and write a paragraph explaining where it lives, what it eats, how it moves, etc.

Insect Riddles

Have the students write riddles about insects, e.g. How do you know that bees watch t.v.? They have antennae. (You may want to read **Creepy Crawly Critter Riddles** or **Bugs** to the class. See Bibliography for publishing information.)

by Redd

Insect Questions

Display pictures of unusual insects along with a supply of insect books and magazines. Encourage students to identify each insect and answer questions such as:

What does it eat? Where does it live? Does it have enemies? What is special about it?

The insect chart on page 24 may be used with this activity.

| Name: | Date: |

Bar Graph

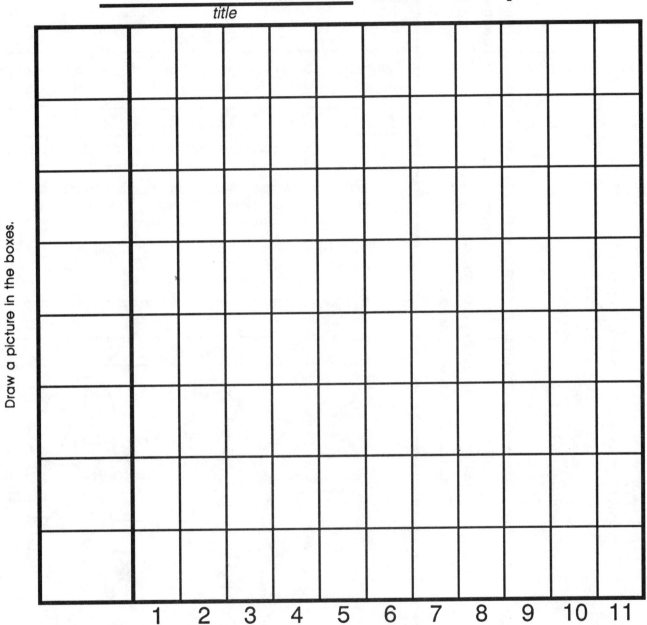

_____
title

Draw a picture in the boxes.

1 2 3 4 5 6 7 8 9 10 11

1. What does this graph show? _____

   _____

2. The favorite choice is _____

3. More students voted for _____ than _____ .

4. I chose_____because _____

   _____

   _____ .

Compound Words Egg Carton Game

Skill: Compound Words

Direction: Pair the words on the bugs to the words in the egg cup bottoms to form the names of twelve different insects. Write them on a sheet of paper.

Extensions:

• Write the names of the insects in alphabetical order.

• Make a list of five more insect names that are not compound words.

• List all the insect names from this game. Next to each one write the number of syllables that it contains.

• Find out about these insects.

Egg Carton Cover

Materials:

egg carton; tape or rubber cement; self-stick colored dots; felt tip marker; scissors.

Directions:

• Cut out the egg carton cover (left) and attach to the outside lid of the egg carton with tape or rubber cement.

• Write a matching answer for each problem on the self-stick dots; press into the egg cup bottoms. You will need to label the dots with the following words:

did	bug	hopper
bee	fish	bear
fly (make 4)	worm (make 2)	

• Cut out game pieces (below). Store them in an envelope in the egg carton.

Game Pieces

katy

glow

dragon

butter

silver

wooly

grass

fire

house

honey

lady

silk

fly

butter

Name:	Date:

Butterfly Treats

These clever butterflies are easy to make and good to eat! But before you begin you must unscramble the **bold** letter groups in the directions below. Use the Word Bank to help you.

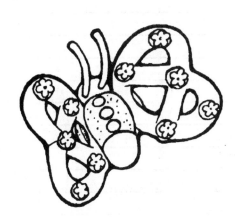

Ingredients:

candied **ranoge** __ _r_ __ __ __ __ slices;

zertples __ __ __ __ _z_ __ __ __;

canned frosting; sprinkles; licorice;

ugm podrs __ __ _m_   __ __ __ _p_ __,

jelly beans, or other **nacdy** __ __ _n_ __ __.

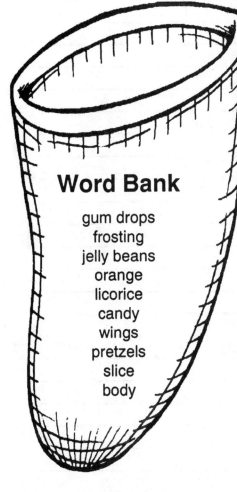

Word Bank

gum drops
frosting
jelly beans
orange
licorice
candy
wings
pretzels
slice
body

Directions:

To make the **doyb** __ __ __ _y_, cut two slits in

a candied orange **lisce** _s_ __ __ __ __.

Press one pretzel into each slit to make **swgni**

__ _i_ __ __ __.

Spread **strofnig** __ __ __ __ _t_ __ __ __ on the wings and body.

"Glue" the **corlicei** __ __ _c_ __ __ __ __ __ and sprinkles to the body to form antennae and details.

Experiment with gumdrops and

llejy snabe _j_ __ __ __ __   __ __ _a_ __ __

to make body parts.

Name:	Date:

An Insect Alphabet

Work with a partner to make an Insect Alphabet. After each letter write two or more words that have to do with insects. Some words are given to help you. Compare lists with other groups.

A antennae

B

C

D dragonfly

E

F

G

H

I

J

K

L

M

N

O

P

Q

R

S sections

T

U

V

W

X Xerces butterfly

Y

Z

Name:	Date:

Bug Wordsearch

Find all the insects listed on the jar lid below in the wordsearch. Words may be across, down, backwards, or diagonal.

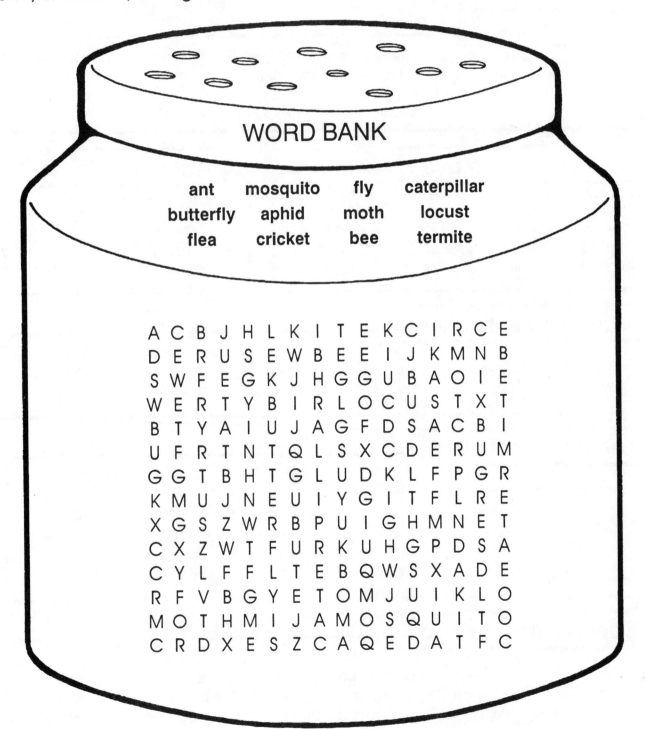

WORD BANK

ant	mosquito	fly	caterpillar
butterfly	aphid	moth	locust
flea	cricket	bee	termite

```
A C B J H L K I T E K C I R C E
D E R U S E W B E E I J K M N B
S W F E G K J H G G U B A O I E
W E R T Y B I R L O C U S T X T
B T Y A I U J A G F D S A C B I
U F R T N T Q L S X C D E R U M
G G T B H T G L U D K L F P G R
K M U J N E U I Y G I T F L R E
X G S Z W R B P U I G H M N E T
C X Z W T F U R K U H G P D S A
C Y L F F L T E B Q W S X A D E
R F V B G Y E T O M J U I K L O
M O T H M I J A M O S Q U I T O
C R D X E S Z C A Q E D A T F C
```

How many times can you find the word BUG? [ ] Circle it in red each time.

41

Insect Word Banks

This resource page is a handy reference for various writing activities such as reports, creative writing, rhymes and poems, social studies lessons, and science experiments. In addition, these words can be used as spelling word lists and can serve as a springboard for brainstorming.

Insect Names

		bee	grasshopper	termite	dragonfly
ant	aphid	fly	stinkbug	cricket	locust
flea	firefly	praying mantis	butterfly	ladybug	wasp
mosquito	moth	beetle	katydid	walking stick	

Ways Insects Move

			crawl
wriggle	fly	swim	dance
scurry	kick	skate	march
dig	paddle	hop	run
jump	walk	dive	wiggle

Insect Noises

chirp	zoom
zip	singing
buzz	snapping
tweet	

Where Insects Live

			under stones	rivers	grass
deserts	houses	trees	gardens	trees	food
sand	clay	forests	other animals	open fields	ponds

Things Insects Do

			gather	build	spin
drink	skip	mate	bite	sting	eat
whorl	burrow	dig	munch	change	hop
dance	shed	fly	prey	damage	jump
trap	molt	crawl	migrate	carve	
skim	hatch	tunnel	chew	loop	

Special Insect Words

		head	abdomen	camouflage
larva	thorax	egg	larva	prey
migrate	pupa	adult	nymph	mimicry
pheromones	antennae	invertebrate	mouthparts	endangered
colonies	cocoon	chrysalis	metamorphosis	hibernate

Making A Venn Diagram

A Venn diagram is an illustration that compares and contrasts two different things. This diagram consists of two overlapping circles (see example below). The overlapping space in the center contains ideas or statements that are true for both things being compared. Each outer circle lists characteristics that belong to one of the items only.

For example, compare moths and butterflies. They are alike because they are insects, have two antennae, undergo metamorphosis, and lay eggs. They are different in many ways: Most moths fly by night, most butterflies fly in the daytime; moths are dull-colored, while butterflies are brightly-colored; moths spin silk, but butterflies do not; moth pupae live in a cocoon while butterfly pupae have a chrysalis. Information like this can be assembled in a more graphic and legible way by using a Venn diagram as shown in the illustration below.

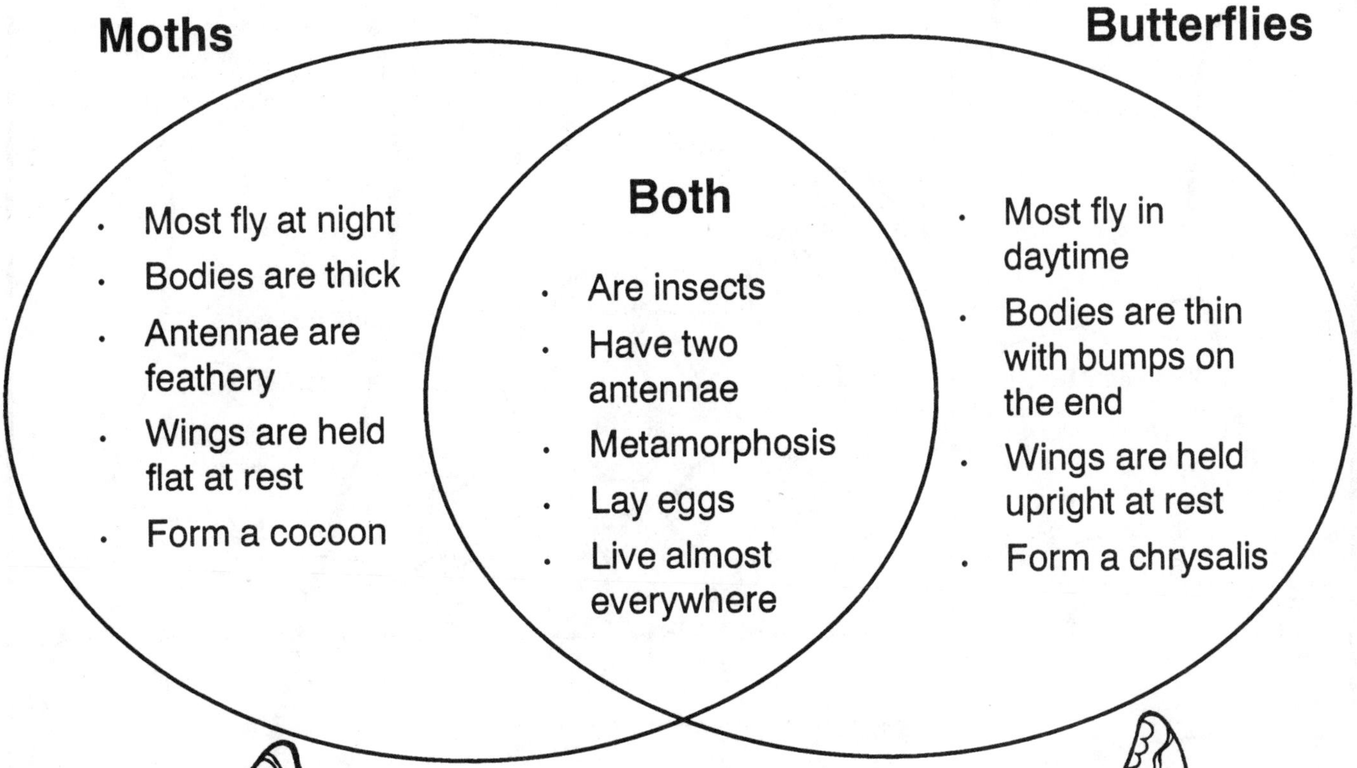

Moths

Butterflies

Both

- Most fly at night
- Bodies are thick
- Antennae are feathery
- Wings are held flat at rest
- Form a cocoon

- Are insects
- Have two antennae
- Metamorphosis
- Lay eggs
- Live almost everywhere

- Most fly in daytime
- Bodies are thin with bumps on the end
- Wings are held upright at rest
- Form a chrysalis

To make a Venn diagram with the whole group, you will need to conduct a brainstorming session in which likenesses and differences are explored. These ideas can be listed on a chart or the chalkboard first and then transferred to the Venn diagram itself. Small groups can work together to complete their own diagrams after they have had practice with the whole group. Some other possible topics to compare besides insects themselves are books; characters from books, plays, or stories; songs, rhymes, or poems; life cycles; habitats.

Math

Ant Gameboard

Directions:

Cut out along the solid outside lines. Glue to tagboard; color and laminate. Cut out the task cards on page 45. Players will each need a marker. The first player chooses a card and answers the question. If his response is correct, he rolls a die and moves that number of spaces. If incorrect, he remains on his space. Play continues until the first one reaches the Finish.

Task Cards

Use with Ant Gameboard, page 44. Glue to tagboard, cut apart, and laminate. To make this game self-checking, write the answer next to its corresponding number on a separate sheet of paper.

1 16 ant's on a log. 7 fell off. How many are left?	**2** 5 ant's. 6 ant's. 2 ant's How many altogether?	**3** 14 ant's. 5 more. How many altogether?
4 4 ant's. 4 cube's (sugar cubes). How many cube's for each ant?	**5** 7 ant's. 11 more. How many altogether?	**6** 4 nests. 2 ant's in each nest. How many ants altogether?
7 20 ant's. 16 went to find food. How many are left?	**8** 3 ant's. 6 kernel's. (corn kernels) How many kernel's each?	**9** 2 ant's. 5 ant's. 5 ant's How many altogether?
10 6 baby ant's. 8 more baby ant's. How many now?	**11** 1 worker ant. 9 worker ant's. 5 worker ant's. How many altogether?	**12** 18 ant's. 12 went to work. How many are left?
13 10 leaf's. 2 ant's. How many leaf's each?	**14** 14 ant's. 3 ant's found food. How many did not find food?	**15** Mother ant Father ant 14 baby ant's. How many in the family?
16 3 ant's. 6 ant's. 8 ant's How many altogether?	**17** 13 ants in the nest. 6 ants went out of the nest. How many ants were left in the nest?	**18** 4 ant's. 4 pea's (peas). How many pea's for each ant?
19 3 ant's at a picnic. 10 more come. How many now?	**20** 2 nests. 10 ant's in each nest. How many ants altogether?	**21** 14 ant's. 3 more. How many now?

Name:	Date:

Insect Math

Add or subtract.

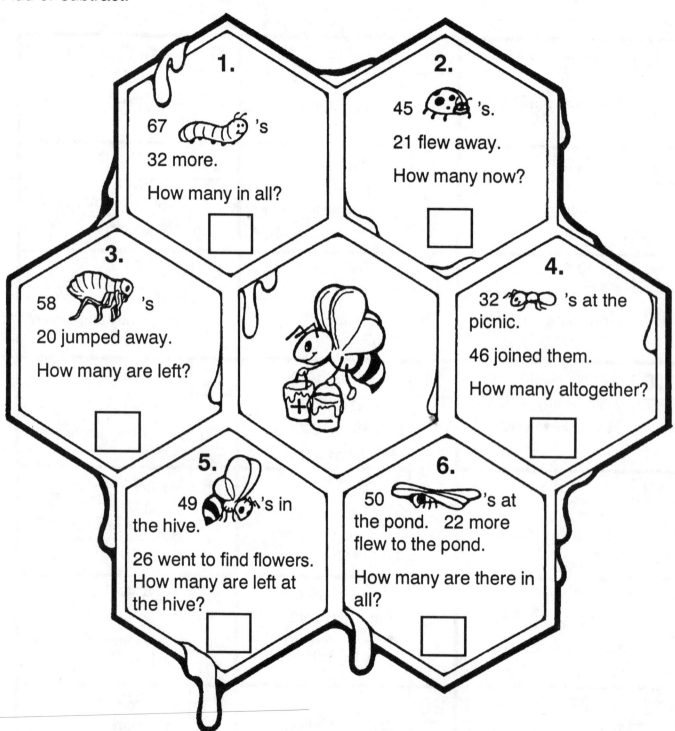

1.
67 's
32 more.

How many in all?

☐

2.
45 's.
21 flew away.

How many now?

☐

3.
58 's
20 jumped away.

How many are left?

☐

4.
32 's at the picnic.

46 joined them.

How many altogether?

☐

5.
49 's in the hive.

26 went to find flowers. How many are left at the hive?

☐

6.
50 's at the pond.   22 more flew to the pond.

How many are there in all?

☐

Name:	Date:

Do You Know These Insects?

Answer each problem below.
Write the letter for that number
in the spaces.

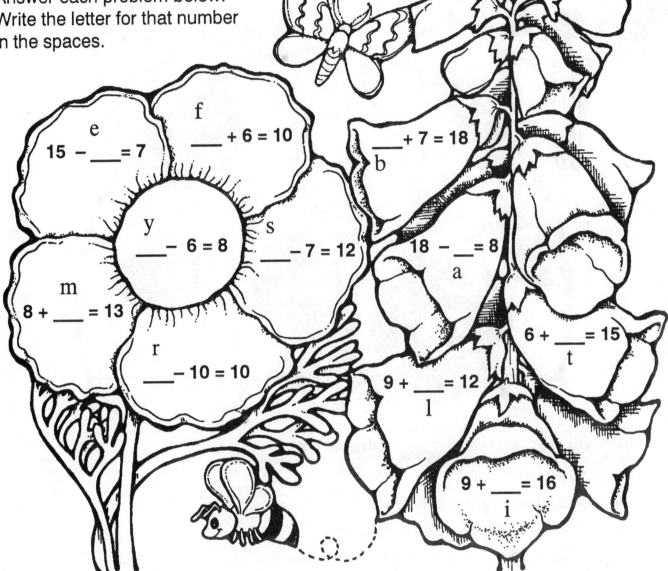

e
$15 - \underline{} = 7$

f
$\underline{} + 6 = 10$

b
$\underline{} + 7 = 18$

y
$\underline{} - 6 = 8$

s
$\underline{} - 7 = 12$

a
$18 - \underline{} = 8$

m
$8 + \underline{} = 13$

r
$\underline{} - 10 = 10$

t
$6 + \underline{} = 15$

l
$9 + \underline{} = 12$

i
$9 + \underline{} = 16$

1. Everywhere it goes, it leaves germs. $\underline{}\ \underline{}\ \underline{}$
   4 3 14

2. This pest likes to eat wood. $\underline{}\ \underline{}\ \underline{}\ \underline{}\ \underline{}\ \underline{}\ \underline{}$
   9 8 20 5 7 9 8

3. It feeds on the blood of cats, dogs, and even humans! $\underline{}\ \underline{}\ \underline{}\ \underline{}$
   4 3 8 10

4. This insect glows in the dark. $\underline{}\ \underline{}\ \underline{}\ \underline{}\ \underline{}\ \underline{}\ \underline{}$
   4 7 20 8 4 3 14

5. They live in hives. They make wax and honey. $\underline{}\ \underline{}\ \underline{}\ \underline{}$
   11 8 8 19

         # 268 Thematic Unit — Creepy Crawlies

Ladybug Pencil Poke

Directions:

- Cut out the ladybug shape.

- Punch holes along the perimeter of the ladybug.

- Write a different problem next to each hole punched.

- Turn the ladybug over and write the answers to the problems next to the corresponding hole.

- Staple two craft sticks together to the bottom of the ladybug placing one stick on each side of the ladybug (see diagram).

To Play:

- One child faces the front of the ladybug while another child faces the back of the ladybug.

- The child facing the front of the ladybug puts a pencil (or golf tee) through any hole and says the problem aloud. (For example, in the diagram above, if the child puts his pencil through the top right hole he would say, "Three plus five equals eight."

- The child facing the back of the ladybug checks the answers.

- After all the problems have been computed, the children trade places.

Name:	Date:

Did You Know...?

Learn some interesting insect facts. First, solve the problem. Then write the answer in the blank. Last, read the sentence.

---

90 + 10=

The African Goliath Beetle is the heaviest beetle in the world. It weighs _____grams or as much as 33 pennies!

---

50 – 20=

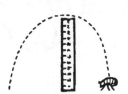

Fleas are very tiny yet they can jump _____ centimeters. That's about the height of this page!

---

300 + 100=

The loudest insect in the world is the male Cicada. He can be heard over _____meters away which is about the distance of four football fields.

---

4 + 2=

Some termites build amazing houses out of dirt. They can be over three meters thick and _____ meters high. That's as tall as a two-story building!

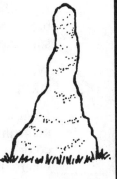

---

20 – 1=

The longest beetle in the world is the American Hercules Beetle. It is _____centimeters long which is about as long as a new pencil.

---

55 – 10=

During its lifetime a worker honeybee collects enough nectar to make _____ grams of honey. It would take six bees their whole lifetime to fill a 12 ounce (355 ml) soda can with honey.

       # 268 Thematic Unit — Creepy Crawlies

Food For Thought

Find out how much of a leaf a caterpillar can eat in one day by following the step-by-step directions in this simple experiment. Afterwards, students may want to test other insects to find out which one eats the most in one day. This experiment can be done in pairs or small groups.

Materials:

A caterpillar; a box (preferably with a screen top); a large leaf; two different colored markers; pencil, copy of graph (page 51).

Directions:

- Place the leaf onto the graph (page 51); trace around the leaf with one of the markers.

- Put the leaf in the box with the caterpillar. Be sure to close the lid of the box.

- **Hypothesis:** A caterpillar can eat between _____ and _____ square centimeters of leaf in one day.

- Wait until the same time the next day to take the leaf out of the box.

- Lay the leaf over the graph tracing you made the day before. Using the other color marker, trace around the places where the leaf has been eaten.

- Fill in the space to show how much leaf is now gone.

- Count the number of squares that are in the area that the caterpillar ate. A square that is more than half covered should be counted as a whole square. But if a square is less than half covered, do not count it at all.

- **Result:** The area eaten by the caterpillar was _____ square centimeters.

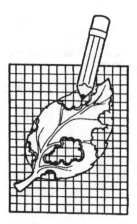

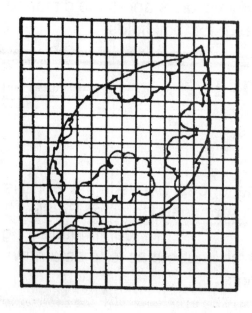

50

Name:	Date:

Graph For Food For Thought

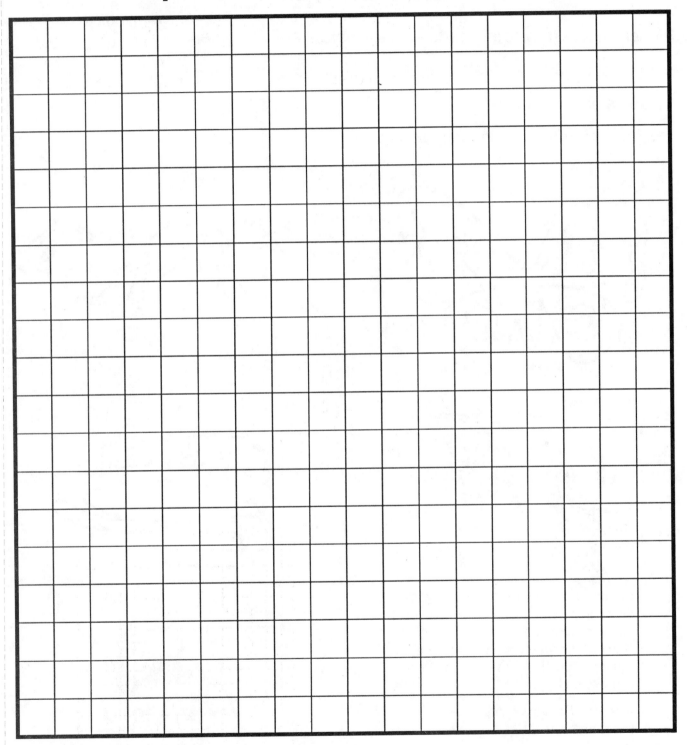

Hypothesis: A caterpillar can eat between _____ and _____ square centimeters of leaf in one day.

Result: The area eaten by the caterpillar was _____ square centimeters.

| Name: | Date: |

Insect Parts

All insects have three body parts—head, thorax, and abdomen.

Some insects have two feelers, or antennae, on their heads.

All insects have six legs.

Draw the missing parts on these insects.

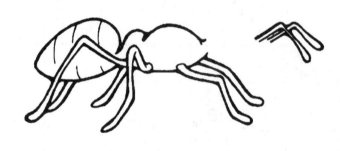

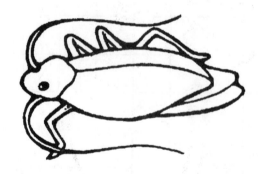

Nom:	Date:

Nomme les insectes

1. trouve les insectes.
2. coupe et colle
3. colorier

une mite	une fourmi	un Papillon	une mouche
coccinelle	une abeille	un scarabée	

Moth Life Cycle Viewer

To help you learn about the life cycle of a moth, make this viewer. First, cut out the cocoon shape on this page; cut out the dashed lines to make a window. Then follow the directions on the next page.

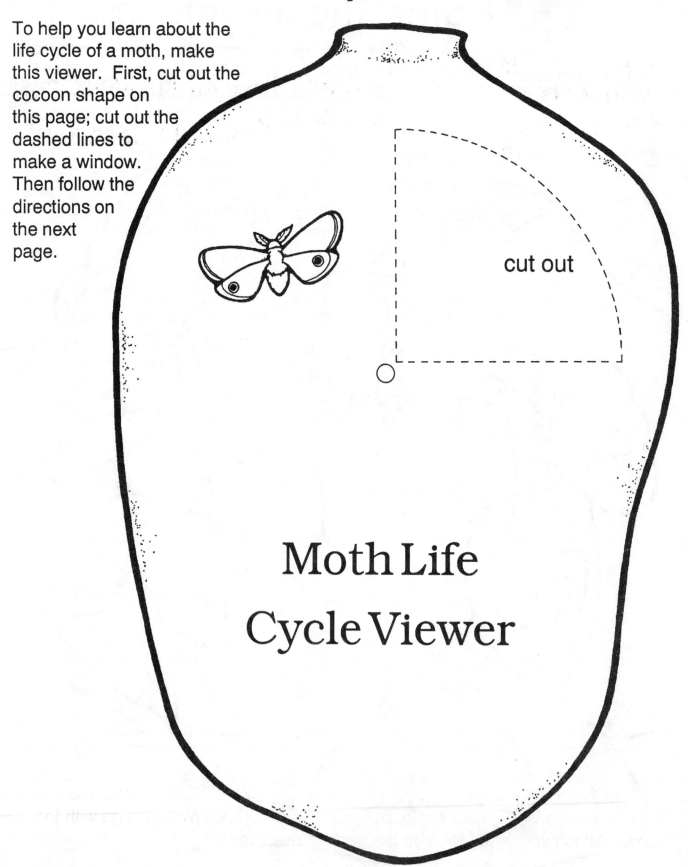

cut out

Moth Life

Cycle Viewer

54

Moth Life Cycle Viewer *(cont.)*

Directions:

Cut out the circle below.

Color the pictures.

Attach the circle behind the cocoon on page 54 with a paper fastener through the center.

Rotate the wheel until the number one picture shows up in the window.

Read the story by moving the wheel clockwise.

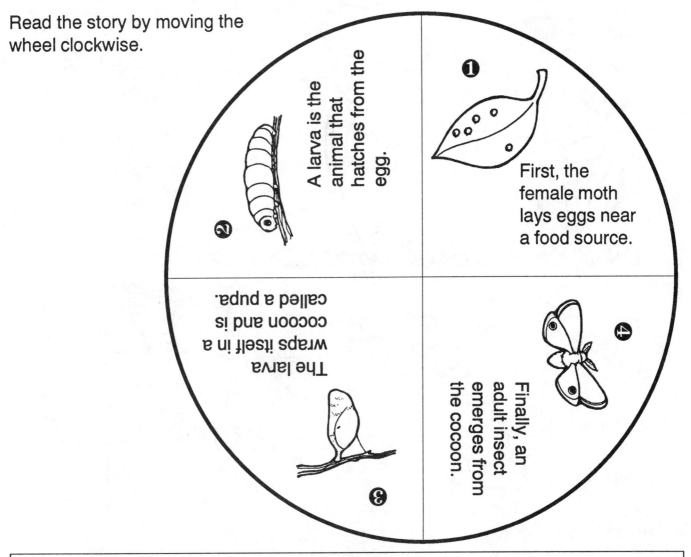

Challenge:

Find another insect that has four changes in its life cycle. Make a circle and divide it in four equal parts. Write a sentence in each part. Draw a picture to go with the words. Attach your story circle to the back of the cocoon.

Name:	Date:

Helpful Or Harmful

Some insects are harmful pests. They bite people, carry germs, or eat things people need. Other insects are helpful because they eat harmful insects or carry pollen which helps plants grow.

Draw a circle around the harmful insects. Color the helpful insects.

Trace the **word**.

Helpful Insects. butterfly   ladybug   moth

Harmful Insects. fly   ants   mosquito

termite   grass

Challenge: Is a bee helpful or harmful? _____

Name: _____   Date: _____

Insect Friends

Some insects sting us. Ouch! Some insects carry germs that make us sick. But some insects are our friends. Unscramble the bold names below and find out how some insects help us. Use the Word Bank to help you.

1. **eBse** ___ ___ ___ ___ make honey and carry pollen.

2. A **tohm** ___ ___ ___ ___ larva spins silk for clothes.

3. **gonfisarDle** ___ ___ ___ ___ ___ ___ ___ ___ ___ ___ eat mosquitoes which can spread diseases.

4. Some **sletbee** ___ ___ ___ ___ ___ ___ ___ eat insects that harm orange trees.

5. **saWsp** ___ ___ ___ ___ ___ carry pollen to plants.

6. A **dylagbu** ___ ___ ___ ___ ___ ___ ___ eats aphids which are harmful insects.

Word Bank

Write each insect name.

bees _____   wasps _____

ladybug _____

dragonflies _____

moth _____   beetles _____

A Graph Art Butterfly

The purpose of a graph art project is to create a picture by coloring the squares on a graph according to given directions. Many learning skills are incorporated in this seemingly simple project: following directions, graphing, directionality, and concentration on a task, among others. It crosses the curriculum as it combines reading, math, art, and language. Furthermore, the finished product provides a child with a sense of accomplishment which enhances his self-esteem. This activity can be done independently or as a group activity guided by the teacher. It is suggested that the first one be done under close teacher supervision to eliminate problems on subsequent pictures. Step-by-step directions follow:

- Give each student a blank graph sheet (page 61) and a copy of the directions (page 60).

- Model how to follow directions. For example, Row 1 might say Color 6 [B] 1 [O/R] 1 [O/R]. This means that the first six squares in Row 1 should be colored blue; the next square should be colored orange in the top left triangle, red in the bottom right triangle; the next square should be colored orange in the top right triangle and red in the bottom left triangle.

- Have students cross out each direction on the direction sheet as it is completed.

- Fold each row back as it is completed.

Helpful Hints

- Have extra graph sheets available; errors may be made on first attempts.

- Direct the students to color the squares solidly and stay within the lines.

- The finished product will be most attractive if the squares are not outlined.

- The project may be extended over several days by doing a row or two per day.

- Show the Answer Key (page 59) to the students **after** they have completed the project.

- For more graph art projects see the Teacher Created Materials book listed in the Bibliography, page 79.

Graph Art Answer Key *(cont.)*

Do not show to students until they have completed the project.

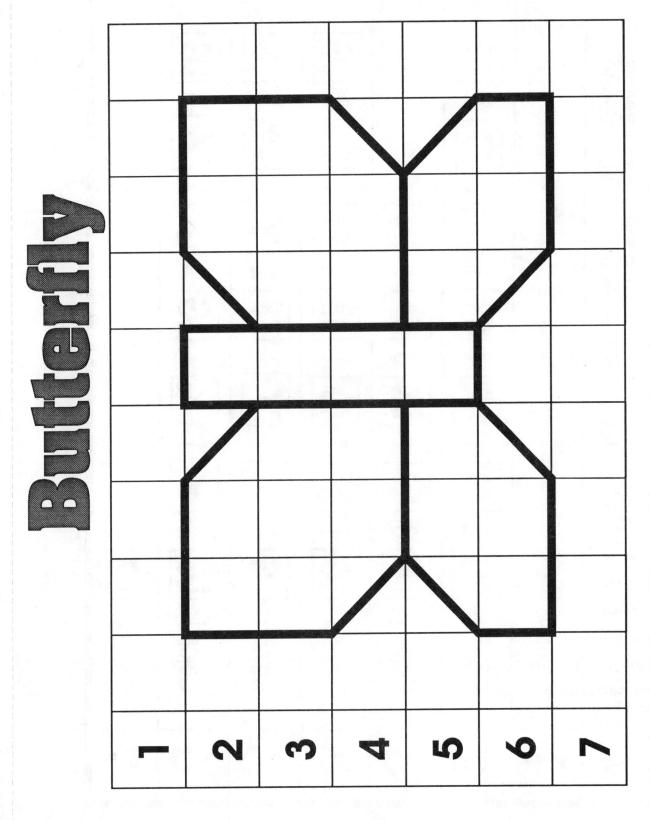

Butterfly

Directions for Graph Art (cont.)

Mystery Picture	Color Key								
	LG = light green Y = yellow O = orange BK = black								
1	Color 9 LG								
2	Color 1 LG	2 O	1 [LG/O]	1 BK	1 [LG/O]	2 O	1 LG		
3	Color 1 LG	3 O	1 BK	3 O	1 LG				
4	Color 1 LG	1 [LG/O]	2 O	1 BK	2 O	1 [LG/O]	1 LG		
5	Color 1 LG	1 [LG/Y]	2 Y	1 BK	2 Y	1 [LG/Y]	1 LG		
6	Color 1 LG	2 [Y/LG]	1 LG	1 LG	2 Y	1 [Y/LG]	1 LG		
7	Color 9 LG								

Blank Graph For Graph Art (cont.)

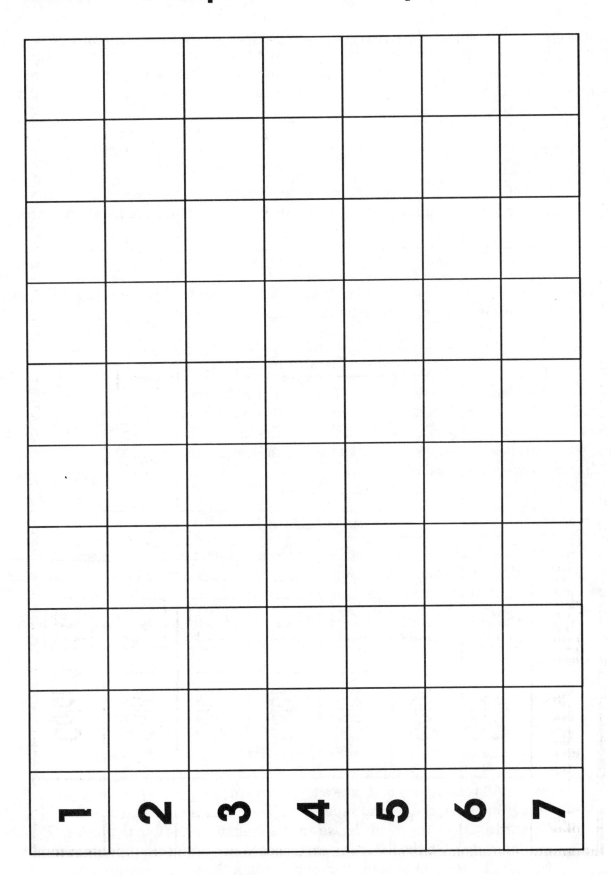

Creative Movement

It is important to include creative movement and music in the primary curriculum because children learn about themselves and their environment when they are involved in these kinds of activities. Furthermore, the use of movement and music fosters cooperative learning and social interaction. The following ideas are presented as guidelines and should be adapted to suit your classroom needs.

Bee Moves

Play a recording of **The Flight of the Bumblebee**. Encourage students to "buzz" around and move like a bee. Or, have the students fingerpaint pictures while they are listening to the music.

Insect Dances

Make masks on pages 63 and 64 (or others created by students). Students may make wings to complete their costumes. Then, work in small groups to create insect dances.

Swamp Obstacle Course

Create a swamp obstacle course. Line up chairs for the children to crawl under. Place a refrigerator box on its side and have the students crawl through it into a small plastic (or inflatable) unfilled wading pool. After everyone has completed the course, have them go through it again in reverse order.

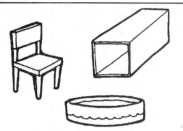

Insect Sounds

Provide students with a variety of musical instruments or objects that could be used to make sounds (pots, metal lids, wooden blocks, etc.) Have students perform the following kinds of movements and sounds:

Buzz like a bee. Chirp like a cricket. Zoom like a dragonfly. Wiggle like a mosquito larva. Jump like a flea. Inch along like a caterpillar. Break out of a cocoon like a butterfly.

Shoo Fly

Teach the students the song "Shoo Fly, Don't Bother Me." Then make up a simple game or dance to go with the words. For example, have everyone hold hands in a circle. All raise hands and take a step forward as they sing the first "Shoo, fly, don't bother me." On the second repetition, lower hands and take one step back. Move forward again on the third phrase and back again on the fourth phrase, "For I belong to somebody." On the following part, choose two adjacent students to form an arch. Choose one student to lead everyone through the arch and into a new circle.

Caterpillar Mask

Directions for Caterpillar Mask:

- Duplicate the pattern on colored paper.
- Glue to tagboard for more durability; laminate if desired.
- Cut out around the whole head.
- Cut out the inner circles to make eye holes.
- Attach two short lengths of pipe cleaners to make antennae.

- Staple a craft stick to the bottom of the mask so students can hold it up to their face.
- Have students make up their own insect dances in small groups and present them to the rest of the class.

Butterfly Mask

Directions for Butterfly Mask:

- Duplicate the pattern on colored paper.
- Glue to tagboard for more durability; laminate if desired.
- Cut out around the whole head.
- Cut out the dotted circles to make eye holes.

- Attach two pipe cleaners to make antennae.
- Staple a craft stick to the bottom of the mask so students can hold it up to their face.
- Have students make up their own insect dances in small groups and present them to the rest of the class.

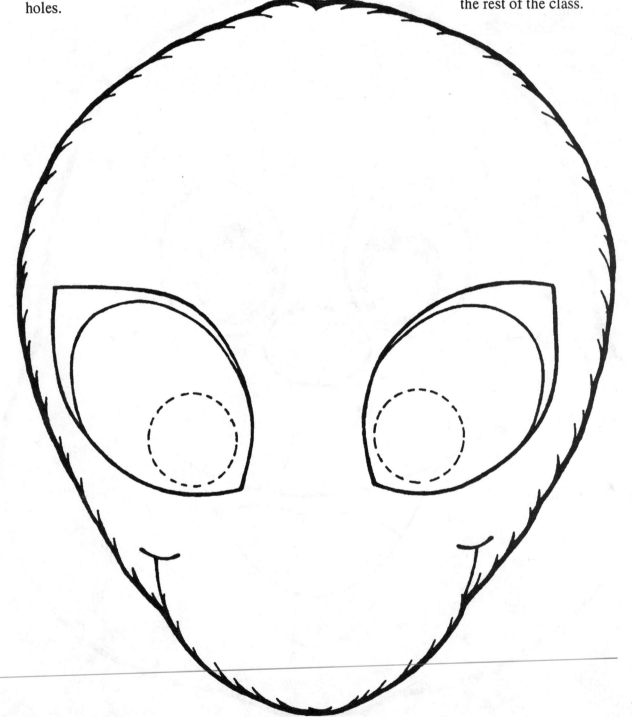

Edible Insects

Here are two easy, fun recipes for insects that are good to eat!

Cute as a Bug Salad

Ingredients:

- Canned peach (or pear) halves; lettuce; raisins; chow mein noodles; cream cheese (preferably whipped); maraschino cherries cut in slices; carrot curls.

Directions:

- Place one peach half on a lettuce-lined plate.

- Attach raisin eyes, maraschino cherry mouth, and chow mein noodle antennae with dabs of cream cheese.

- Place carrot curl legs around the peach half body. (To make carrot curls, use a vegetable peeler to peel wide strips from the carrot. Roll up each strip; fasten with a wooden toothpick. Place the curls into a bowl of ice water for several minutes. Remove toothpicks before placing them around the peach half.)

Bug Bites

Ingredients:

- Prepared cookie dough; decorating goodies such as nuts, raisins, coconut flakes, mini semisweet chocolate pieces, dry cereal, canned frosting, sprinkles.

Directions:

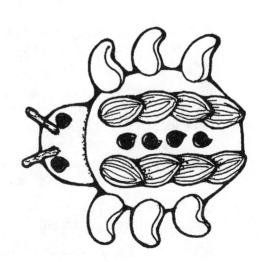

- Spoon the cookie dough onto a sheet. With your fingers press the dough into an insect shape.

- Decorate the shape with any of the suggested goodies, above.

- Bake as directed.

- Cool on a wire rack. Then enjoy!

Very Important Insects

End your Insect Unit with a presentation for parents, another class, or the principal. Have students give short reports and afterwards serve refreshments. Complete directions are given below.

- Read *The Important Book* by Margaret Wise Brown (Harper and Row, 1949) to the class. Suggest an insect and then brainstorm why it is important; list all the reasons on the chalkboard or on chart paper.

- Assign or have each student choose an insect to write about.

- Use the language pattern from *The Important Book*.

Important Book Language Pattern

The important thing about _____ is
that _____.

It _____

It _____

It _____

It _____

It _____

It _____

But the important thing about _____ is that it is
_____.

- After the written assignment has been completed, do an art project to go with the words. Students can draw, paint, make clay models, make a collage (see page 67 for directions), construct a mobile, or make 3-D models (see page 67 for directions) of their insects.

- In small groups make refreshments for those who will be attending. Some menu ideas are tea with honey and biscuits; honey treats (see page 67 for directions); Cute as a Bug Salad (see page 65 for directions).

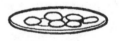

- Send invitations (see page 77 for samples). As a class, compose an invitation letter. Have each child copy the letter onto their invitation stationery.

- On the day of the presentation set up a table with refreshments, napkins, paper cups, or any other supplies. Make sure that students have their texts and illustrations ready.

- Afterwards, display the Very Important Insect pages and projects on the walls.

Very Important Insects *(cont.)*

Collage

Materials: Construction paper, crayons or markers; scissors; glue; assorted decorative items such as toothpicks, glitter, buttons, beans, pipe cleaners, colored tissue, cotton swabs, cotton balls, foil, fabric, etc.

Directions:

- Have the student draw an outline of an insect on a sheet of construction paper.
- Encourage the student to decorate the insect picture with any of the materials available.
- Cut around the insect after decorating, if desired.

Honey Treats

Ingredients: 1 cup (240 ml) peanut butter (unsweetened smooth or chunky style); 1 cup (240 ml) powdered milk; 1/2 cup (120 ml) honey; 1 teaspoon (5 ml) vanilla; 1/2 cup (120 ml) raisins.

Directions:

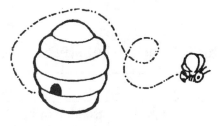

- Mix all the ingredients together in a large bowl.
- Roll the dough into 1 inch balls.
- With the bottom of a drinking glass, flatten each ball slightly.
- Place on wax paper on a cookie sheet.
- Chill. Store covered in refrigerator.

Makes about 4 dozen.

3-D Models

Materials: 12" (30 cm) pipe cleaners; construction paper; glue; one-hole punch; scissors.

Directions:

- Hold two pipe cleaners together about a thumb's length from the top and twist them together four or five turns.
- Take one of the long loose ends and bring it up and fasten it to the top of the turns.
- Repeat with the other side.
- Bend the pipe cleaners to make wings; bend the untwisted ends to make antennae or a head.
- Cut two pieces of construction paper to fit the wings; glue to the bottom of the pipe cleaners.
- Turn over the insect shape.
- Cut two pieces of a different color construction paper to fit on the top wings.
- Punch out holes on the paper.
- Glue the paper wings to the front of the pipe cleaners.

- Additional lengths of pipe cleaners may be added to make other features.

Caterpillar's Story

Objectives:

This interactive bulletin board can be used to teach the life cycle of the butterfly.

Materials

- colored construction or butcher paper
- scissors
- stapler
- thick green craft yarn
- pushpins

Construction

- Reproduce patterns onto appropriately colored construction paper and cut out.
- Assemble all pieces onto the bulletin board background; attach with staples or pushpins.
- Make as many branches as you need. Attach to tree.
- Attach the bags, butterflies, etc. as directed on pages 6 and 7.
- Add a pond and grass if you would like.

Directions

- Use to enact the butterfly life cycle (see pages 6 and 7).
- Display insect art projects or pictures on the bulletin board. Add grass, a pond, rocks, and other geographical features. Place the insects in their proper habitats.

Attach branches (page 71) here.

Caterpillar's Story Bulletin Board *(cont.)*

Attach on top of Tab A page 70.

TAB A

Caterpillar's Story Bulletin Board *(cont.)*

Caterpillar's Story

Bulletin Board

TREE BRANCHES

Make as many as needed.
Attach to the tree trunk.

Caterpillar's Story Bulletin Board *(cont.)*

ROCK

Caterpillar's Story Bulletin Board *(cont.)*

CATTAILS

Awards

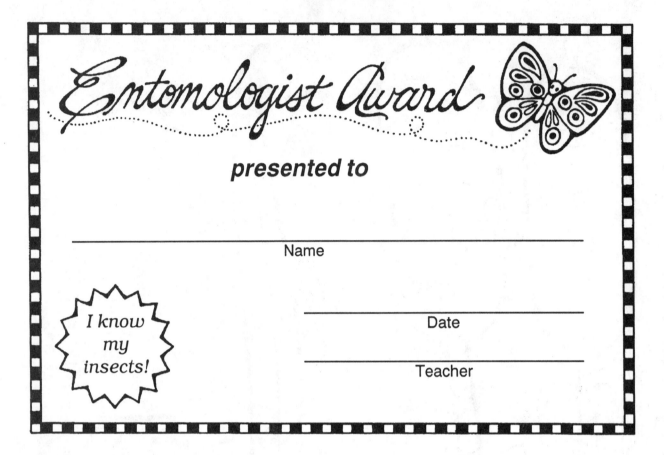

Entomologist Award

presented to

_____

Name

I know my insects!

_____

Date

_____

Teacher

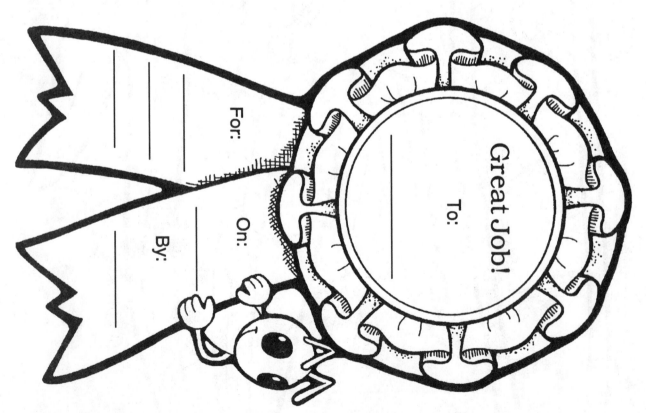

For:

On:

By:

Great Job!

To:

Clip Art

Stationery

Unit Management

Learning Center Record Form

NAME	Activity										

Bibliography

Fiction

Aardema, Verna. *Why Mosquitoes Buzz in People's Ears*. Dial Press, 1975

Aesop's Fables. Avenel Books, 1912

Berstein, Joanne E. and Cohen, Paul. *Creepy Crawly Critter Riddles*. Weekly Reader Books, 1986

Brown, Margaret Wise. *The Important Book*. Harper and Row, 1949

Carle, Eric. *The Grouchy Ladybug*. Harper and Row, 1977

Carle, Eric. *The Very Hungry Caterpillar.* Putnam, 1969

Garelick, May. *Where Does the Butterfly Go When It Rains?* Scholastic, 1961

Geraghty, Paul. *Over the Steamy Swamp.* HBJ, 1988

Lionni, Leo. *Inch by Inch*. Astor-Honor, 1962

Lobel, Arnold. *Fables.* Harper and Row, 1980

Lobel, Arnold. *Grasshopper on the Road.* Harper and Row, 1978

Pallotta, Jerry. *The Icky Bug Alphabet Book*. Charlesbridge Publishing, 1986

The Random House Book of Poetry for Children. Random House, 1983

Van Allsburg, Chris. *Two Bad Ants*. Houghton Mifflin, 1988

Nonfiction

Better Homes and Gardens Crazy Creatures. Meredith Corporation, 1988

Better Homes and Gardens Bugs, Bugs, Bugs. Meredith Corporation, 1989

Braithwaite, Althea. *Butterflies.* Longman Group USA, Inc., 1977

Gibbons, Gail. *Monarch Butterfly.* Holiday House, 1989

Heller, Ruth. *Chickens Aren't the Only Ones.* Grosset and Dunlap, 1981

Kaufman, Joe. *Slimy, Creepy Crawly Creatures.* Western Publishing Co., Inc., 1985

Kilpatrick, Cathy. *Creepy Crawlies.* US Borne First Nature Books, 1982

Parker, Nancy Winslow and Wright, Jean Richards. *Bugs.* Mulberry Books, 1987

Reidl, Marlene. *From Egg to Butterfly.* Carolrhoda Books, Inc., 1981

Seymour, Peter. *Insects: A Close Up Look.* Macmillan Publishing Co., Inc., 1984

Whalley, Paul. *Butterfly and Moth.* Alfred A. Knopf, 1988 (An Eyewitness Book)

Teacher Created Materials

095	*Simple Graph Art*
217	*Creepy Crawlies for Curious Kids*
228	*All About Science Fairs*
229	*Problem-Solving Science Investigations*
301	*Literature Activities for Young Children, Book 2*
311	*Literature and Critical Thinking, Book 12*
355	*Literature and Critical Thinking, Book 1*

Answer Key

Page 17

1. six
2. three
3. two; two

Page 25

Alike

1. starving
2. fearful
3. hungry
4. sneaky
5. unfriendly
6. surprised

Opposite

1. friendly
2. generous
3. alert
4. lazy
5. full
6. tiny

Page 39

Ingredients: orange, pretzels, gum drops, candy.

Directions: body, slice, wings, frosting, licorice, jelly beans

Page 45

1. 9
2. 13
3. 19
4. 1
5. 18
6. 8

7. 4
8. 2
9. 12
10. 14
11. 15
12. 6
13. 5
14. 11
15. 16
16. 17
17. 7
18. 1
19. 13
20. 20
21. 17

Page 46

1. 99
2. 24
3. 38
4. 78
5. 23
6. 72

Page 47

1. fly
2. termite
3. flea
4. firefly
5. bees

Page 49

1. 100
2. 400
3. 19
4. 30
5. 6
6. 45

Page 57

1. bees
2. moth
3. dragonfly
4. beetles
5. wasps
6. ladybug

Page 41

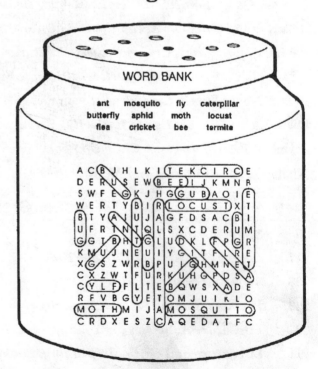

bug- 7 times